Financial Innovation
AI in Banking, Investing, and Risk Management

Table of Contents

Chapter 1. Introduction

SPECIAL REPORT: Financial Innovation: AI in Banking, Investing, and Risk Management

In an ever-changing financial ecosystem, navigating the complex world of banking, investing and risk management is a task that requires continuous learning and quick adaptation. Welcome to our Special Report on Financial Innovation where we probe into a game-changing aspect of financial services today: Artificial Intelligence. Fear not the technical complexity. Delivered in an effortlessly understandable format, this report puts forth an eye-opening narrative exploring how AI is not simply transforming banking and investing operations but is also revolutionizing risk management strategies. By simplifying the intricate, we aim to equip you with the knowledge that takes you ahead of the curve, effortlessly demystifying the complexities of AI in the financial sector. Whether you are a professional or a curious mind, this report is guaranteed to enlighten, inform and inspire you. Get ready to unlock unprecedented insights that chart the path for the future of finance.

Chapter 2. The Vanguards of Change: Artificial Intelligence in Finance

Market trends, customer needs, and technological advancements coalesce in finance more dynamically than ever before. This intersection heralds a new era where Artificial Intelligence (AI) emerges as not just a disruptive force but as vanguard of change, upending traditional models and redefining approaches to banking, investing and risk management.

2.1. AI and the Banking Transformation

The advent of AI has facilitated a rapid digital transformation within the banking sector. Starting from frontline interactions with customers to back office operations, AI has imprinted its influence in every aspect of banking, enhancing speed, efficiency, and personalization.

AI-powered chatbots automate customer interactions, thereby enabling quicker response times and 24/7 availability, without sacrificing the quality of customer service. By analyzing customer data, chatbots even offer personalized financial advice, leading to a more engaging customer experience.

Back-office operations have also noticeably benefitted from AI. Machine learning algorithms, substantially reducing the number of manual tasks, facilitate automatic processing of data, error detection, and corrections. Fraud detection has also markedly improved, with AI tools identifying suspicious patterns with much more accuracy and speed than human-involved processes.

AI's influence also manifests in credit scoring. No longer a simplistic approach, AI is used to probe beyond credit histories. By analyzing vast amounts of non-traditional data like social media activity and online transactions, AI provides a more accurate and comprehensive measure of an individual's creditworthiness.

2.2. AI in Investment: A Paradigm Shift

Investment strategies today bank on AI with a remarkable frequency. Automating labor-intensive tasks, AI is rapidly changing the face of portfolio management, high-frequency trading, and algorithmic trading.

Robo-advisors, intuitive AI-powered platforms providing automated, algorithm-based financial planning services, are a testament to this shift. Performing a range of functions, from portfolio rebalancing to tax-loss harvesting, robo-advisors cater to lower-capital investors, democratizing access to investment advice.

High-frequency trading (HFT) and algorithmic trading are also increasingly employing AI. Able to process vast amounts of data at blistering speeds, AI supports these trades by predicting market changes, identifying trading opportunities, and executing trades in microseconds.

AI's inherently predictive abilities allow for forecasting market trends with a higher degree of accuracy. By considering a wide array of variables, including global news, economic indicators, and social media sentiment, AI heralds a more data-driven, efficient approach to investing.

2.3. The Fortification of Risk Management with AI

Conventional risk management strategies often struggle to cope with the evolving financial landscape. Herein lies AI's invaluable contribution, shoring up risk management with its predictive analytics, real-time insights, and scenario simulations.

AI models offer robustness and speed that have revolutionized credit risk assessments. AI sifts and analyzes enormous quantities of data, providing risk scores that factor in a wide spectrum of variables - from credit history to purchasing behaviour.

In the same vein, AI has transformed operational risk management. Machine learning algorithms detect anomalies, predict potential difficulties, and alert risk managers in real time, allowing for a proactive approach towards risk mitigation.

For a sector as volatile as finance, AI's blessings extend to market risk management. By employing AI for scenario simulations and predictive modelling, financial institutions can assess the impact of various market fluctuations on their portfolios and make informed decisions.

2.4. The Road Ahead: AI Ethics in Finance

As majority financial institutions tread along the path of unprecedented AI integration, issues of transparency, fairness, bias, and privacy loom large. Developing ethical AI mechanisms, which not only enhance competitiveness but also uphold the principles of fairness and transparency, is a looming challenge that the finance sector needs to confront.

The rise of AI in finance is not an evolutionary step, but a revolution; with AI being the vanguard rather than an engine of change. Its impact is wide reaching and salutary. However, this promising future can only be realized with a grounded understanding of what AI can and cannot do. It is only with this clear understanding that a path for the successful integration of AI in finance can be carved out. Banks and financial institutions need to stay abreast with the latest in AI to ensure the technology enriches their operations and customer interactions, and helps them manage the ever-perplexing risks that suffuse this dynamic landscape that is the financial sector.

And thus, with AI at the helm, the finance sector can step confidently into an exciting, transformative future that promises not just prosperity, but a high degree of efficiency, effectiveness, and inclusivity.

Chapter 3. Decoding AI: Understanding the Basics

Artificial Intelligence, commonly known as AI, is an umbrella term for technologies and processes that enable machines to mirror human intelligence. This mirror reflects various human cognitive functions such as comprehension, decision-making, problem-solving, and learning. It has been a subject of fascination and exploration, leaving an indelible impact on numerous aspects of human life, not least in the realm of banking, investing, and risk management.

3.1. What Exactly is AI?

While understanding AI, it's useful to begin with the broadest perspective. According to the father of AI, John McCarthy, it is "the science and engineering of making intelligent machines, especially intelligent computer programs". In essence, AI involves developing computer systems that are able to perform tasks involving human intelligence. This includes speech recognition, decision-making, visual perception, language translation, and even problem-solving.

Formally, AI is categorized into two types - Narrow AI and General AI. Narrow AI, often called weak AI, is designed to perform a specific task, such as voice recognition. It is the form of AI that we see all around us today - in search engines like Google, digital assistants like Siri, and recommendation algorithms on Netflix and Amazon.

General AI, on the other hand, often called strong AI, is an AI system with generalized human cognitive abilities implying that when presented with an unfamiliar task, it has the ability to find a solution on its own. Currently, general AI is aspirational and serves as a motivating goal for AI research.

3.2. How Does AI Work?

The primary tool that allows us to unlock the potential of AI is data. Machines that are powered by AI harness patterns and information from the data to improve their operation, allowing them to learn from past experiences and anticipate future outcomes. This is achieved through several methods, with machine learning and deep learning being the most commonly used.

Machine learning (ML) is a subset of AI, where computer algorithms improve automatically through experience. It uses statistical techniques to enable machines to improve with experience.

Deep learning, a subset of machine learning, uses artificial neural networks to simulate human decision-making. It's based on the premise of neural networks in the human brain, processing data in layers and making decisions.

AI technologies can take context into consideration, allowing for more personalized experiences. For instance, they can understand the nuances in human speech, consider online browsing behavior while presenting targeted ads, or even detect fraudulent activity in financial transactions.

3.3. AI in Computing and Processing Information

A key process of AI technologies is computing and processing a massive amount of data for meaningful output. AI-powered systems can process vast amounts of information, identify trends and patterns, and make data-driven decisions. The expansive capabilities help in analyzing large datasets that are beyond human capabilities.

For instance, in financial forecasting, AI can process large volumes of historical data to predict future trends. Similarly, in banking, AI algorithms can analyze thousands of transactions in real time to monitor for fraudulent activities.

With their superior speed and accuracy, AI systems greatly exceed human capacity and efficiency. They enable automating routine tasks, thus reducing the need for human intervention and risk of errors.

3.4. Evolution and Advancements in AI

The concept of AI has been around for quite some time. However, advancements in AI have achieved significant momentum in the last few decades, thanks to increasing computational power, new methodologies, and the availability of large datasets.

Major breakthroughs have come on the back of innovations in machine learning—such as reinforcement learning—and deep learning, like convolutional neural networks (CNNs) and recurrent neural networks (RNNs). These technologies have made it possible to build AI systems that can handle complex tasks with a high degree of accuracy.

Recent years have also seen the advent of 'explainable AI' or XAI. The aim here is to make AI decision-making transparent and comprehensible to humans, which is crucial in highly regulated sectors like finance and healthcare.

3.5. Conclusion: The Road to AI Maturity

In conclusion, to truly leverage the power of AI, it's imperative one has a solid understanding of its basics. Embarking on this AI journey entails comprehending what AI is, how it works, its uses, and the advances being made in this pioneering field. Armed with this foundational knowledge, individuals, businesses, and society at large are better prepared to navigate the promises and challenges that AI holds for us.

AI is as much a tool for the present as it is a promise for the future. As with any tool, understanding its workings paves the way for optimal use. With AI, this understanding could lead to breakthroughs and advancements that redefine the world of finance, creating a landscape that's efficient, secure, and full of potential. As AI moves from fledgling to maturity, through a focus on ethics and explainability, we are set to witness transformative impacts in banking, investing and risk management. The journey of understanding AI is akin to decoding the DNA of this transformation.

Chapter 4. AI in Banking: Transformation Triggered

In the realm of digital transformation, artificial intelligence (AI) has hit the ground running and banking is no exception. With its potential to redefine the relationship between banks and customers, AI is augmenting functionalities, catalyzing strategic growth, and triggering a transformation like never before.

4.1. AI Driven Banking: An Overview

Artificial Intelligence in the banking industry essentially refers to advanced machine learning algorithms that are capable of learning from experiences, predicting future outcomes, and making complex decisions in real time. This heralds a new era of banking where routine tasks are taken over by automation, advanced analytics guide decision-making and the entire banking ecosystem is interconnected, agile, and customer-centric.

Bringing wide-ranging benefits to both businesses and customers, AI is now more than just a technological innovation – it is a key driver of operational efficiency, growth, and competitive advantage in the banking sphere.

4.2. Exploring the Potential of AI in Banking

When it comes to banking, AI creates value in three major ways: 1) By improving customer experience through personalization, immediate response, and 24/7 accessibility, 2) By enhancing operational efficiency through process automation and risk analytics, and 3) By facilitating risk management through predictive analytics and real-time detection of fraud or cyber threats.

AI's direct impact on banking can be seen in the areas of customer service, process automation, and data analysis. For instance, AI-powered chatbots and virtual assistants are now delivering personalized, intuitive services round the clock while machine learning algorithms are enabling banks to optimize operations, reduce errors, and minimize costs.

4.3. AI and Customer Experience

Artificial intelligence allows banks to deliver a hyper-personalized customer experience. By harnessing predictive analytics, banks can anticipate customer behavior, understand individual preferences, and offer tailored products and services. AI-powered chatbots, for instance, are already extending real-time support and services to customers, even providing financial advice based on their spending habits and financial goals. Moreover, voice recognition technology facilitates biometric authentication, ensuring swift, secure, and seamless transactions.

On the other hand, AI-driven neural networks enable sentiment analysis, allowing banks to respond to customer needs more effectively, thus enriching customer relationships.

4.4. AI and Process Automation

Process automation driven by AI is not just about cutting costs; it's about driving operational efficiency and making banking seamless. By automating routine tasks, AI frees up human resources for more strategic, compensation-earning tasks. Robotic Process Automation (RPA), AI's subset, allows for the automation of repetitive tasks, leading to increased productivity, reduced manual errors, and improved compliance.

However, AI's role goes beyond RPA: it streamlines workflows, reduces false positives in fraud detection, and aids in decision-making through pattern detection and predictive analytics.

4.5. AI and Data Analysis

Big data is the new oil, and AI is the rig tapping into it. In a data-driven banking universe, AI and machine learning are powering real-time analytics, driving insights that help banks make informed decisions. Fraud detection, credit risk analysis, and customer segmentation were once laborious, manual tasks. Today, AI is transforming them into intelligent, predictive, and automated systems.

More than just number-crunching, AI systems sift through vast data lakes, spotting trends and patterns that remain elusive to the human eye. This leads to more accurate risk assessments, proactive fraud detection, and smarter marketing strategies.

4.6. Real World Applications and Case Studies

From global banking behemoths to innovative fintech start-ups, the application of AI in banking is varied and vast. For example, JPMorgan Chase uses an AI program, COIN, for document review and contract intelligence, saving thousands of man-hours. Similarly, American Express uses AI to analyze more than a billion transactions, identifying purchasing behaviors, and potential fraud.

Furthermore, fintech disruptors like Ant Financials are taking AI adoption a notch higher, deploying AI across their services – from wealth management to loan processing – injecting speed, accuracy, and efficiency.

4.7. Conclusion: The Road Ahead

AI in banking is just beginning to unfold. From a nascent experiment, it has evolved into a strategic imperative, pushing banks to reimagine their models, operations, and customer engagement. While implementation is fraught with challenges – from data privacy issues to integration complexities – the rewards far outweigh the risks.

As banks gear up for the AI revolution, the key is to strike a balance between automation and human touch. The future of banking isn't just machine-led; it's a seamless fusion of human and AI capabilities that build trust, drive growth, and craft an experience that's personalised, proactive, and alert at all times.

Chapter 5. Robo-Advisors and AI: Revolutionizing Investing

The era of technological advancement in the finance industry spearheaded by Artificial Intelligence (AI) has ushered in exciting innovations, one of the most prominent ones being Robo-advisors. Robo-advisors are automated platforms using sophisticated algorithms to provide financial planning and investment services with little to no human intervention. They are designed to simplify investing, reduce costs, and democratize access to financial advice. Shifting from the conventional advisory model, robo-advisors are reshaping the financial landscape by providing efficient and affordable solutions.

5.1. How Robo-Advisors Work

At their core, robo-advisors transform user inputs regarding financial objectives, risk appetite, and time horizon into a tailored portfolio of investments. Users typically begin their journey by responding to a questionnaire, feeding into the robo-advisor's algorithm that then recommends an optimal asset allocation plan. This recommendation might span a diversified mix of stocks, bonds, real estate, and other asset classes. Robo-advisors manage and adjust the portfolio over time, in response to changes in the market or in the user's financial situation.

Robo-advisors reap the benefits of AI and machine learning. By using big data analytics, robo-advisors can predict market trends, identify investment opportunities, and even learn from investors' behavior patterns. They offer tools for tax-loss harvesting, automatic rebalancing, and risk assessment, providing users with a comprehensive, automated investment management solution.

5.2. The Efficiency of Robo-Advisors

Robo-advisors offer an impressive level of efficiency. Compared to traditional financial advisors, robo-advisors can process enormous quantities of data far quicker. This enhanced quantitative assessment capability enables robo-advisors to offer detailed portfolio analyses and forecasts, providing greater precision and consistency in their advice. Furthermore, having an automated platform managing investments means emotions are removed from the equation, avoiding any human bias or error.

Another benefit is the added convenience. Robo-advisors are accessible 24/7, allowing investors to access their finances on their terms. The automation of mundane tasks, such as portfolio rebalancing and dividend reinvestment, provides flexibility and promotes user engagement, forging a new kind of relationship between investors and their financial advisors.

5.3. Affordability and Accessibility

Traditionally, receiving bespoke financial advice required an investor to have substantial assets. However, this gatekeeping has been disrupted by robo-advisors. Robo-advisors often have low minimum investment requirements or none at all, making them accessible to a broader demographic. Moreover, they tend to charge lower fees than human financial advisors, thereby democratizing access to financial advice and making investing reachable for a larger population.

5.4. The Shortcomings and Risks

Despite the many advantages, robo-advisors have limitations. For one, their algorithms might fail to encompass personal subtleties or the investor's unique life events. In situations requiring personalized advice and emotional intelligence, human advisors may hold an edge. Also, robo-advisors operate under the assumptions of their algorithms, which may not always foresee certain market scenarios or changes in economic indicators. This can lead to systemic risks if several robo-advisors adopt the same flawed algorithms, potentially creating a precarious financial situation.

Another concern is security. As these platforms handle sensitive financial information, safeguards must be in place to protect against cyber-attacks. In this sense, robust and continually updated security measures are vital.

It is also worth noting that, while robo-advisors are excellent at offering short-term tactical adjustments based on algorithms, they may fall short in delivering comprehensive long-term financial planning that entails strategizing around retirement, insurance, and estate planning.

5.5. The Future Prospects

Looking ahead, robo-advisors show significant potential for further development. Integrating elements of behavioural finance into their algorithms is one likely progression, helping investors make more rational investment decisions. In the long run, AI advancements may improve robo-advisors' predictive analytics and personalization capabilities, further disenfranchising traditional financial advisory services.

In the interim, a hybrid model, combining the best of human and robo-advisory, could offer a compelling compromise. Such a system would have robo-advisors managing routine tasks, while human advisors address complex financial planning issues, combining efficiency and precision with personalized advice and empathy.

The advent of robo-advisors and their substantial impact on democratizing investment speaks to the immense potential that lies at the intersection of finance and technology. Although challenges persist, the benefits that robo-advisors bring to the table cannot be ignored. Their rise signals a transformative shift within the financial advisory industry, one that is sure to reshape the landscape of investing in the future.

Chapter 6. AI and Risk Management: New Perspectives

The introduction of Artificial Intelligence (AI) has not only revolutionized operational systems and customer engagement strategies in the financial sector but has also profoundly transformed risk management procedures.

6.1. The Evolution of Risk Management with AI

Risk management has always been a critical aspect of the financial sector. The element of risk is inherent in all banking, investing, and financial operations. Traditionally, these risks have been managed through manual processes and statistical methods. However, with the advent of AI technologies, risk management has taken a quantum leap forward. AI allows for fast, accurate risk assessment and prediction, enabling finance institutions to manage and mitigate risks more effectively. AI's machine learning algorithms can analyze vast quantities of data in real-time, picking up patterns and trends that can signal potential risks, many times before they occur.

AI, particularly machine learning and deep learning algorithms, enables the financial institutions to automate the risk-management process, mitigating the chance of human error. For instance, AI-powered tools can accurately predict patterns of fraud, enabling financial institutions to take preventive measures in real-time. Further, AI can improve operational efficiency by automating routine risk-related tasks, freeing up human resources for more sophisticated work requiring human judgment and discretion.

6.2. Enhanced Predictive Capabilities

AI excels at identifying patterns within complex systems, especially in large datasets where conventional statistical methods falter. Machine learning algorithms feeding on historic data continually adjust their models in the light of new information, allowing these models to 'learn' and make more accurate predictions over time. This ability gives financial institutions an unparalleled ability to preemptively identify potential risks and take remedial measures well in advance.

In banking, models trained on customer behavioral data can predict unusual behaviors signaling credit defaults or fraudulent transactions. In investment scenarios, AI helps manage portfolio risk by accurately predicting market trends, providing desirable risk-reward trade-offs.

6.3. AI in Fraud Detection and Prevention

AI has proven to be an invaluable tool in the fight against financial fraud. AI systems, aided by machine-learning algorithms, can sift through heaps of transactional data flagging unusual patterns that might indicate fraudulent activities. Furthermore, advanced AI techniques such as anomaly detection can identify unusual patterns or outliers that might represent undiscovered fraud, even when such fraud doesn't align with known fraudulent patterns.

AI systems are not only adept at detecting possible fraud; they also excel in determining the likelihood of future fraudulent activities by continually learning and adjusting to new fraud techniques. Consequently, financial institutions are better prepared to handle both emerging and established threats to their operations.

6.4. Operational Risk Management

AI also plays a significant role in managing operational risks, which arise from failures in systems, processes, or people. AI systems can analyze workflow, identify bottlenecks, inefficiencies, or human errors that increase operational risk. AI techniques like natural language processing (NLP) and semantic analysis can help comprehend regulatory texts, identifying compliance risks, and offering mitigation strategies.

By incorporating AI technology, financial institutions can boost the efficiency of their risk management efforts, leading to significant cost savings, enhanced regulatory compliance, and improved overall operational efficiency.

6.5. AI and Cybersecurity in Financial Institutions

Data breaches and other cybersecurity risks have proliferated with the rise of digital banking. To fortify the defense against such attacks, AI steps in as both a protector and a predictor. By analyzing data patterns, AI tools can spot potential vulnerabilities, predict attack scenarios, and initiate preventive measures. Techniques like machine learning and deep learning facilitate the detection of anomalies and make predictive models to stretch the possibilities of cybersecurity from mere protection to robust prediction and prevention.

6.6. The Ethical and Regulatory Considerations

As AI becomes increasingly integral to risk management in finance, it is important to address the ethical and regulatory implications associated with its use. Regulatory bodies are concerned about the lack of transparency, or 'black box' nature, in AI decision-making processes. Some critics argue for the need for an explanation of how AI technologies arrive at certain decisions, especially given the potential consequences for individuals and businesses. Despite these ongoing debates, AI is indispensable to the modern financial landscape and will invariably shape the future of risk management.

In conclusion, AI provides a multi-faceted approach to risk management in the financial sector. As we progressively rely more on AI for key financial operations, the sector will only stand to gain from the superior predictive and analytical capabilities it brings, provided ethical measures and regulatory concerns are duly addressed. AI's future in financial risk management, though complex and fraught with challenges, is ultimately promising and upward bound.

Chapter 7. Exploring AI-Driven Financial Products and Services

The advent of Artificial Intelligence in the world of finance has changed the game on multiple levels, achieving what was hardly thinkable just a decade ago. AI-powered products and services are overhauling the traditional, human-centered financial operations, making them faster, more efficient, and most importantly, more accurate.

7.1. Evolution of AI-Driven Financial Services

It's essential to understand how AI-driven financial services evolved through time. Previously, financial institutions relied heavily on manual data analysis, with human analysts playing a critical role. However, this process was laborious, time-consuming, and prone to errors. At the turn of the century, technology began to automate many of these processes, saving time and reducing the potential for error.

However, the real shift began with the introduction of AI into the finance arena. As computer processing power increased and data storage costs decreased, it became increasingly feasible to apply complex algorithms and machine learning models to huge volumes of financial data, creating the necessary environment for today's AI-driven financial services.

7.2. AI and Banking Services

The influence of AI in banking is vast. The sector, which is widely known for its conservative approach to innovation, has felt revolutionary impacts from AI integration. AI has brought about the advent of chatbots which significantly enhances customer service. By automating answers to frequently asked questions and providing 24/7 support, banking institutions can now serve customers better and faster with reduced operational costs.

Further, AI algorithms assist in fraud detection, spotting unusual transactional patterns that would have taken human analysts a significant amount of time to identify. With AI, detection of fraudulent activities is quick, improving the security of banking transactions.

7.3. AI in Investment Services

Next in line is the effectiveness of AI in investment services. Investment firms and hedge funds are utilizing AI to develop sophisticated predictive models that assist in making trading decisions based on data patterns. AI algorithms analyze vast amounts of financial data and provide valuable insights, empowering investors to make informed decisions and anticipate market trends with great accuracy.

Robo-advisors, fueled by AI, have become standard in the investment industry. They can manage portfolios, rebalance assets, and provide investment advice based on individual risk tolerance and financial goals, all at a fraction of the cost of a human financial advisor.

7.4. AI-Driven Loan and Credit Services

AI is redefining loan and credit services. Before AI, credit decision-making was largely based on human discretion. Today, AI algorithms can predict an applicant's default potential by analyzing an immense array of data points, ranging from credit scores to social media activity. This predictive ability enhances financial institutions' confidence in their decisions, thereby improving the transparency and efficiency in the credit services sector.

In addition, AI-driven automation in the loan servicing processes is increasing efficiency by reducing processing time and effort, eliminating paperwork, and speeding up loan disbursement.

7.5. AI in Insurance Services

Insurance companies are leveraging AI in multiple ways. From automating damage assessments in auto insurance through image recognition to utilizing machine learning models for predicting disease onset in health insurance, AI has upended insurance industry norms. AI is also aiding in fraud detection and risk assessment, making underwriting better informed, faster, and more efficient.

7.6. Pushing the Boundaries: The Future of AI in Finance

With the tremendous potential AI holds, the future of finance is replete with possibilities. The merging of AI with other advanced technologies, like blockchain and IoT, could enhance predictive analysis, increase transaction security, and create a trove of novel services tailored to specific customer needs. Moreover, the integration of AI with big data can reveal unprecedented insights that will help financial institutions offer better products, services, and customer experiences.

In conclusion, AI's integration in the financial sector has revolutionized not only the way the industry operates, but how consumers interact with financial services. The adoption of AI-driven financial products and services not only indicates a massive paradigm shift for the industry but also sets the path for a technologically-advanced, more efficient future in finance. As sophistication in AI algorithms and technology grows, so too will its influence on the world of finance.

Chapter 8. Ethical and Regulatory Challenges: AI in Finance

Artificial Intelligence (AI) has brought immense transformation to the financial sector, introducing new opportunities and challenges in its wake. As the industry continues to digitize and AI applications increase, so does the requirement of regulatory bodies to have a more in-depth understanding of these technological advancements. More so, setting alignment between mechanized intelligence and ethical standards is crucial. In exploring the depths of this conversation, we dissect the foundational ethical and regulatory challenges that AI in finance presents.

8.1. Understanding AI Ethics in Finance

To start, when analyzing AI ethics in the financial sector, it is important to understand its nature. AI comprises algorithms that learn from and make predictions or decisions based on data. The challenge lies primarily in ensuring that these algorithms work effectively without infringing on individual's rights or perpetuating harmful biases.

AI systems, especially deep learning models, are often known as "black boxes." Their decision-making process can be complex and opaque. Furthermore, the larger the database and the more complex the model, the harder it is to interpret the underlying mechanics. This raises the concern of intelligibility and transparency of the AI systems. It can be difficult for human operators - let alone the regulators and consumers - to understand how a particular AI-based decision has been made. In cases where a decision may have adverse effects, such as a rejected loan application or high insurance premium, the lack of explainability becomes a challenge.

Another area of concern is data privacy. AI systems require vast amounts of data to operate efficiently. The collection, use, and storage of such data pose ethical challenges, especially if sensitive personal information is involved.

Moreover, bias in AI systems could lead to unfair outcomes or discrimination. The financial services industry has a complex history with discrimination and bias, and it is essential to ensure that AI systems do not perpetuate or exacerbate these issues.

All these areas contribute to the discussion on ethical considerations surrounding AI use in the financial sector. To address them, we need robust ethical frameworks that guide the development, deployment, and use of AI in finance.

8.2. Regulatory Challenges in AI Adoption

As financial institutions integrate AI into their systems, they face new dimensions of regulatory challenges that add layers of complexity to compliance.

One of the main regulatory challenges concerns the fairness and accountability of AI applications. In several instances, there arises a question on whom to hold responsible when an AI system makes a wrong decision or causes harm. Is it the developer, the user, the institution, or the AI itself? This challenge calls for clarity on regulations regarding responsibility and liability.

Different countries and regions also have different regulatory environments, with differing attitudes towards AI in finance. This makes it challenging for financial businesses operating across borders, as they need to navigate and adhere to multinational legal landscapes, adding to the complexity in establishing universal regulatory and operational standards.

Another challenge comes with auditing. The conventional auditing processes might not suffice for these frontier technologies. How should auditors approach AI? Do they need an understanding of Machine Learning techniques and data science to properly evaluate AI systems? Can they be sure they are dealing with reliable, lawful, and ethical applications of AI?

8.3. Proposed Solutions and Recommendations

Given the ethical and regulatory challenges associated with the integration of AI in the financial sector, several solutions can be proposed.

For ethical issues, raise awareness of AI and its effects among stakeholders including consumers, employees, and regulators. Further, the development of international ethical guidelines for AI applications can help ensure that they are used responsibly.

Regular audits conducted by third parties with expertise in AI can add credibility and ensure compliance with ethical and legal standards.

As for regulatory challenges, governments themselves have a key role to play in creating regulatory frameworks for financial AI that consider aspects of transparency, fairness, data protection, and privacy. Greater international collaboration will facilitate the development and harmonization of legal standards across countries.

In conclusion, the integration of AI in the financial sector presents several ethical and regulatory challenges which, if not handled properly, could lead to infringements on individual rights, bias, and other issues. Understanding these challenges, coupled with robust ethical codes and regulatory guidelines, will help ensure that the use of AI in finance is both beneficial and safe for all stakeholders involved.

While it is not a silver-bullet solution, fostering a mature AI ethics and regulatory environment within the financial ecosystem is a step towards ensuring that as we sail into this new era of digital finance, we do so without compromising the principles that have held us steady in the wake of change.

Chapter 9. Innovative Solutions: Case Studies in AI Transformation

Artificial Intelligence is proving pivotal for financial institutions and companies seeking to stay on the cutting edge. In this chapter, we delve into an array of illustrative case studies that highlight the real-world application and benefits of AI in finance. Our aim is to present thought-provoking examples that manifest the transformative potential of AI in the intricacies of the financial world.

9.1. AI-empowered Fraud Detection: The PayPal Case

In an environment where online transactions are on the surge, detecting and preventing fraudulent activities is a daunting challenge. PayPal, a leader in the electronic payments space, leverages AI to curb fraudulent transactions remarkably. PayPal's deep-learning system scrutinizes each transaction across its vast network in real-time, looking for signs of abnormal activity. By processing vast quantities of data to identify patterns, this technology improves the firm's ability to differentiate between legitimate and fraudulent transactions, reducing false alarms and promoting customer confidence. Such intelligent use of AI has propelled PayPal's standing as a safe platform for online transactions.

9.2. Enhancing user experience: The JPMorgan Chase Example

One of the world's largest financial institutions, JPMorgan Chase has embraced AI to elevate its customer interactions. In a competitive landscape where providing seamless user experience can be a differentiator, the bank introduced COiN, a Contract Intelligence platform that uses machine learning to analyze legal contracts and documents. What would take hours of human labor with potential inconsistencies is now done in seconds with machine precision. This boosts not just efficiency but also customer responsiveness, placing the firm a step ahead of its competition.

9.3. Automating Portfolio Management with AI: ROBO Global's Approach

ROBO Global, a pioneer in robotic and automation investment, leverages algorithmic investing powered by AI for its exchange-traded fund (ETF). Using AI, ROBO Global identifies industries and companies at the forefront of technology and automation. These are analyzed thoroughly on various parameters before including them in the fund. With a low expense ratio and automated rebalancing, this approach takes the guesswork out of investing and delivers consistent returns.

9.4. AI in Credit Risk Assessment: The Case of ZestFinance

ZestFinance, an AI software for credit, employs machine learning to refine its credit-decisioning models. The result is more inclusive and may reduce biases in loan approvals. Recognizing that traditional methods of credit assessment leave out many potentially credit-worthy applicants, ZestFinance harnesses big data to include more nuanced aspects like payment histories for utilities, which aren't typically considered but can be indicative of creditworthiness.

9.5. Improving Trading with AI: The CircleUp Example

CircleUp, a venture capital platform, uses a machine learning classifier named 'Classifier' to identify top-performing consumer companies before their industry breakout. It is trained on extensive private company data and uses that training to make informed decisions on potential investments, giving CircleUp a competitive edge in picking winners. AI-driven approaches like these are transforming how trading and investments are made.

These varied instances represent the breadth of AI applications in the financial world. From fraud detection to customer interactions, portfolio management, credit risk assessment, and trading, AI's transformative potential is clear. As these methods become more commonplace, the financial sector will continue to evolve around the principles of speed, accuracy, and efficiencies driven by AI. For anyone in, or interested in finance, understanding how AI can transform operations is integral to staying relevant in an increasingly digitized landscape.

Chapter 10. Future Projections: Where is AI Taking Banking and Investing?

Artificial Intelligence (AI) has already made significant inroads in the banking and investment sectors, dramatically altering how these industries function. From streamlining operations, improving customer service, to enhancing risk management, AI's applications are broad and varied. The question that remains is: what are the future projections? Where is AI taking banking and investing?

10.1. Utilizing Automation and Machine Learning in Banking

AI, through automation and machine learning, is transforming the operational landscape of banking. Banks are increasingly integrating AI algorithms into their routine operations to enhance efficiency, and this will continue to trend in the coming years. These operations include customer authentication, document verification, fraud detection, and intelligent wealth management, to name a few.

AI's potential lies in its ability to draw insights from big data sets, recognizing patterns, and making outcome predictions. Banks access vast amounts of data daily, and AI analytics can perform in-depth data analysis that can drive optimized decision-making. AI can predict customer behaviors\, improving customer relationship management and targeting.

Now and in the foreseeable future, banks and financial institutions will invest heavily in AI-powered RegTech solutions. Regulatory

Technology (RegTech) can automate the monitoring and management of regulatory compliance, reducing the burden of meticulous manual work.

10.2. Enhanced Personalization in Wealth Management

Personalization will shape the future of wealth management, with AI playing a pivotal role. We are experiencing a shift from mass-market investment products to personalized investment strategies. AI?based robo-advisors are providing tailored financial advice based on individual goals, risk tolerance, and time horizon.

Automated Portfolio Management, or Robo-advisory services, offer algorithms that can execute trades with high frequency and precision, eliminating human errors. Investors receive optimized and real-time financial advice, improving their decision-making. AI will continue to drive hyper-personalization in the wealth management industry, potentially replacing traditional advisors with data-driven, machine-learning based financial advice in the future.

10.3. The Rise of AI in Risk Management

AI is not only reshaping operational procedures and wealth management strategies but also transforming risk management in banking and investment sectors. Financial institutions have to manage complex risks, including operational risk, credit risk, market risk, among others. Traditionally, risk management was a time-consuming and labor-intensive task. Now, AI is easing this burden.

Machine learning models can predict risk outcomes better than traditional models by processing vast sets of data. These models can analyze historic risk events, identifying patterns and assessing the probability of future risk. This enables banks to take pre-emptive measures, reducing risk implications drastically.

AI's ability to detect and predict fraud will shape the future of risk management. Machine learning algorithms can recognize unusual patterns or trends in transactions, flagging potentially fraudulent activities. In the era of increasing cyber threats, with AI, financial institutions can reduce exposure and limit liabilities.

10.4. AI and Banking: The Broader Ethical Implications

As AI continues to infiltrate banking and investing, organizations must be mindful of ethical implications. AI raises important questions around privacy and decision-making. For instance, how should institutions handle sensitive customer data used in AI deployments? Who is responsible in cases where AI algorithms make decisions harming customers or investors?

To navigate these ethical waters, banks and investment firms will need to develop robust frameworks to govern AI deployment. Transparency, accountability, and privacy should be the cornerstones of these frameworks. Moving forward, we can expect increasingly robust regulatory measures to govern AI's role in the banking and investment sectors.

10.5. Conclusion: The Emergence of an AI-incorporated Financial Sector

The future projections for AI in banking and investing are nothing short of revolutionary. AI's ability to automate, analyze, and predict will redefine these sectors' landscape, making them more efficient, responsive, inclusive, and customer-centric. However, along with these advancements come new challenges that need addressing, especially ethical concerns related to data privacy and accountability.

As we move forward, one thing is for certain: AI's role in banking and investing will only grow more profound. Banks, financial institutions, and investment firms need to be prepared to adapt to the demands of an AI-integrated world.

This detailed perspective on AI's future impact on banking and investing encapsulates the complexities and myriad possibilities this technology presents. As we herald the digital revolution in financial services, the exploration of the potential, challenges, and ethical implications of AI will be the key to shaping a sustainable and inclusive financial future. Whether a seasoned finance professional or a curious reader, understanding AI's role in the financial sector can empower you to be part of this evolution.

Chapter 11. Putting It All Together: Leveraging AI for Financial Success

As we plunge further into the digital age, Artificial Intelligence (AI) has progressively ingrained itself within major economic sectors, paving the way for transformative and disruptive innovation. The financial services industry, encompassing banking, insurance, investment, and risk management, is no exception to this technology-fuelled transformation. AI's capacity for data analysis, prediction, automation, and personalization is altering service delivery models, enhancing decision-making processes, and shifting the entire financial landscape. Let's delve into the integration of AI-powered tools and applications within the financial sector and how they can be leveraged for financial success.

11.1. The Force That Is AI

Harnessing the power of AI implies accepting the raw grunt, precision, and instrumental transformative potential it carries. In essence, AI underpins two key machine learning branches: supervised, with its ability to anticipate future events based on past data, and unsupervised, adept at uncovering unknown patterns within datasets. Both variants have utilized financial data to power predictive analytics, personalization, process automation, risk management, and customer engagement.

Despite advanced AI systems providing a remarkable level of utility, it needs high-quality data as input. Data is fundamental in training these models and ensuring their accuracy rates are satisfactory. Therefore, financial institutions must prioritize data management and ensure the accuracy, quality, security, and privacy of data for AI to function optimally and deliver meaningful outputs.

11.2. Overhauling Customer Interactions

Customer interactions encompass a broad spectrum of activities, from account setup and simple transactions to more complex ones, like loan applications or wealth management advice. Traditionally, these transactions entailed lengthy wait times and stringent bureaucratic processes. AI algorithms and chatbots now streamline these processes, imbuing efficiency, personalization, and accuracy.

Robo-advisors, for instance, are revolutionizing investing by offering personalized, low-cost investment advice based on AI's predictive capabilities. Chatbots and virtual assistants, on the other hand, drive client support services, accessing account information, answering routine questions, and providing investment advice anytime, anywhere, at unprecedented response times.

11.3. Amplifying Risk Management

Risk management has traditionally been a labor-intensive and time-consuming effort, demanding painstaking attention to detail. AI has the potential to revolutionize this space by introducing prediction capabilities and automating long-winded processes.

Through machine learning, pattern recognition, and natural language processing, AI can analyze vast amounts of data to predict market trends and behaviors. This enables financial firms to anticipate and mitigate potential risks more efficiently. Cognitive computing also enhances fraud detection through real-time analysis of credit card usage and other transactions, highlighting any deviation from regular patterns that could indicate fraud or cybercrime.

11.4. Supercharging Trade and Investment

Trading is one realm where AI has already demonstrated its worth. High-frequency trading powered by AI, for example, can execute thousands of orders at speeds far beyond human capability. Moreover, AI systems can analyze market trends and data patterns to predict price movements, directing investment strategies that boost profits and reduce losses.

Robo-advisors, with their in-depth analysis and prediction capability, can guide investment decisions by evaluating risk tolerance and investment objectives against market trends. Further, AI's sentiment analysis can evaluate patterns in market sentiment to inform investment decisions, thereby optimizing returns.

11.5. Redefining Compliance and Regulatory Practice

Regulatory compliance ranks high among challenges faced by financial service providers, with the cost of compliance engagement and violation penalties being considerable. Deploying AI means financial institutions can automate the monitoring process to spot deviation from regulatory standards, thereby ensuring adherence and minimizing the risk of non-compliance.

Automating routine tasks within regulatory and compliance monitoring systems can free up significant resources, allowing firms to focus on strategic decision-making and risk mitigation. Even as global regulations become more rigorous, AI can facilitate regulatory reporting and even predict potential future regulations based on historical trends.

No overview of AI in the financial sector would be complete without acknowledging the challenges it presents. These include data privacy and security concerns, regulatory hurdles, reliance on high-quality data, job displacement fears, and the risk of systems making decisions beyond human control. Nevertheless, with a structured approach to AI adoption, these challenges can be minimized and should not detract from the transformative potential AI brings to the financial sector.

The integration of AI in banking, investing, and risk management has begun to transform these fields. It's a trend that will continue to accelerate as we venture further into the digital age and as AI technology continues to evolve. Participants in the financial sector, whether they are individuals, financial institutions, or service providers, who understand and utilize this technology will be the likely beneficiaries in the era of AI-powered finance. Not merely a harbinger of efficiency and accuracy, AI has demonstrated its potential to be a powerful ally in navigating the complex, fast-paced world of finance. It's an exciting era, and the doorway to unprecedented financial success lies wide open for those ready to embrace it.

www.ingramcontent.com/pod-product-compliance
Lightning Source LLC
Chambersburg PA
CBHW062306290526
45794CB00006B/2713